How YOU Can Make Money Blogging from Home

The Ultimate Beginner's Guide to Turning Your Passion for Blogging into Paychecks Using Proven Strategies, Tips, and Tricks

By Millie Loralie

The author of this book has taken careful measures to share vital information about the subject. May its readers acquire the right knowledge, wisdom, inspiration, and succeed.

Table of Contents

Introduction

Congratulations on downloading this e-book! We would like to extend our warmest gratitude for choosing us to assist you in your blogging journey.

The following chapters will teach you the ins and outs of blogging, and everything that you need to know about creating and managing a profitable blog.

Chapter 1 discusses the basics of blogging. It is vital to build a good base before you begin, so that you have a better understanding of what blogging really is, as well as to be informed about terminology and what goes into a blog.

Chapter 2 talks about the effective ways to make money with your blog. This is the key to generate profits, which can eventually lead to financial freedom.

Chapter 3 explains the ways you can draw traffic to your blogs, such as by taking advantage of social media and other outlets that promote blogs like yours.

Chapter 4 shares a number of tips and tricks that can significantly increase your chances of success. In the world of blogging, these are must-know tips that every successful blogger uses.

Chapter 5 shows you how to take what you have learned and apply it to your own blog.

The number of books available on this subject are vast so, thank you again for choosing ours! Every effort was made to ensure it is full of as much useful information as possible. Please enjoy!

Chapter 1: Blogging Basics

A blog is your personal space online. It is like a diary that you can share with the world, where you can share your thoughts, ideas, and stories. A blog has endless possibilities; it can be about whatever you want, and you can talk about anything to your heart's content. For example, do you like poetry? Come up with a poetry blog where you can post and share your poems with an audience. Those who like to travel create a travel blog where they write about their experiences, the do's and don'ts of traveling, and other helpful tips that may assist other travelers. There are also those who write about love and share their experiences with romance and heartbreak, while others come up with beauty and fashion blogs that share the latest fashion trend and make recommendations to their readers. As they say, "The sky is the limit." and blogging is no exception. Find your passion, and share it with the world!

Another remarkable thing about blogging is that it is not only a place for you to express yourself and share ideas with people, it can also be used to generate money! In fact, there are bloggers who earn a full-time income with their blogs. Hence, having a blog can be a good way to escape the rat race to the office, perhaps even leading to financial freedom.

Why People Read Blogs

People read blogs for a whole multitude of reasons. Understanding why someone wants to read your blog is so important to your success. The number one reason is to be informed. For example, if a person wants to learn more about running, he would look for blogs on running. Most of your visitors will come to your blog for information. However, this is not always the case. Others will read blogs just for entertainment. Hence, they go to blogs that have some comedy or humor. These blogs may not have anything serious or meaningful about them, but people still visit them to get a good laugh. Some people read blogs as a way to feel not so alone. There are bloggers who share their personal life, and people usually follow these kinds of blog either because they feel like they have the same or similar experience, or simply because they like the author of the blog. As you can see, there are many reasons why people read blogs. The important thing is that you understand why people will want to read YOUR blog, and to understand the power of your blog to make human connections.

Is It for You?

It is true that anyone can blog, but it is not something that is suitable for everyone. This is because blogging takes a lot of time and effort, especially if you intend to make it into a source of income. You need to come up with new content and updates almost daily for your blog. This is where the problem usually arises. There are people who want to have a successful blog but, may not have the time or motivation to continually update one. If you want to have a successful blog, a blog that can generate a regular stream of profits, you should know that you need to dedicate serious time and effort to creating content. You absolutely need to update your blog on a regular basis, with at least one fresh article or post every week. You also need to promote your blog to an audience. Of course, you are not obliged to post new content on your blog. In fact, there are people who simply abandon their blog and only come back to it when they have some free time. However, the problem with this kind of approach is that the blog will usually fail to generate a regular flow of readership. In other words, it also fails to earn any profit. Take note that the more time and effort that you put into your blog, the more successful it will become.

Why Start a Blog?

The reason a person may blog can be vast. Some like to blog just for the sheer enjoyment of it. It might be OK to update content on your blog to share with others every once and a while for this reason. If you do decided to blog to make a profit, it will involve spending countless hours working on and researching content to generate money. It is possible to earn quite a bit of money simply by blogging. It is also a good way to meet people who share the same interest as you.

How to Start a Blog?

If you think that you have what it takes to be a successful and engaging blogger, then it is time for you to learn how to create a blog, which is the easiest part. Just stick to the steps in this book, and you will have a blog that will grow an audience and revenue in no time.

Choose your blogging platform

There are many blogging platforms available online that will allow you to create and manage a blog. How can you tell which one will best suit your needs as a blogger? More than 70% of bloggers recommend WordPress, and is the top choice for professional bloggers. One of the best things about using WordPress is that you can customize every part of your blog. Not to mention, it has many templates and designs that look sleek and professional.

The only issue a beginner blogger might have with WordPress is that it is a bit more complicated to use compared to other platforms. You need to have a bit of understanding of HTML and other coding programs. No need to fret; you do not have to be a professional programmer to use WordPress. There are many guides online, even on YouTube, that will show you how to use WordPress.

If you want a blog that is simpler to manage, then the number one choice would be Blogger. Blogger is owned and managed by Google, so you can be sure that it can be trusted. Blogger is so easy to use that even if you do not know how to use any HTML, you can still come up with a beautiful and well-designed blog. It offers a blogging platform that is highly intuitive and simple to use.

By doing a search online, you can find many other platforms for blogging, such as Weebly, Wix, and others; but WordPress and Blogger remain the top choices by professional bloggers in the blogging industry. When deciding on the blogging platform that you will use, it is also important to use a platform that has well-established credibility, so there is no concern when the platform might suddenly close down at any time.

Host your blog

Blog hosting is important to allow you to run and manage a blog. If you just want to test the water or simply want to blog as a hobby, then you can host your blog by using any of the free platforms for blogging. Both WordPress and Blogger offer free blogging platforms. However, the problem with hosting your blog using a free platform is that you do not get to have your own domain name. You only get a sub-domain. Hence, your blog URL will contain .wordpress or .blogspot (if you use Blogger). So for example your website domain name might be "www.thisismyblog.wordpress.com", instead of getting your own domain name, in which case it could be "www.thisismyblog.com". If you are really serious about blogging, then it is strongly recommended that you host your own blog. Hosting your own blog is as fast and easy as creating one. The cost of hosting a blog is also quite affordable.

There are many available services online that you can use for hosting a blog. One of the most recommended services is BlueHost. In fact, even WordPress itself promotes BlueHost for all blogs and websites. Therefore, if you are a WordPress user, then BlueHost may just be your number one choice.

If you intend to rake in serious profits with your blog, then you should definitely consider hosting your own blog. Otherwise, your blog will look unprofessional with a sub-domain appearing on your URL. It is hard for people to treat you seriously if you do not even spend a small amount of money to host your blog. The cost of hosting a blog is usually lower than $25 per year.

Domain name

Your blog's domain name is important. Naming your blog is like naming a person. Take note that you cannot change your domain name unless you transfer your blog to another domain — which is not a recommended method. It is advised that your domain name should have a word or title that will reflect what your blog is about so that people will know what to expect from you. For example, if your blog is about music, then you can use the word *music* as part of your domain name so that people will have an idea as to what to expect from visiting your blog. Using a generic term that relates to your blog is also one of the ways to increase your blog's SEO ranking. This means that it can drive more traffic to your blog.

There are, of course, exceptions. There are bloggers who do not use any generic name as part of their domain name. In fact, you will not get any hint as to what their blog is about just by reading their domain name. They are still able to turn it into a successful blog.

Although your blog's domain name does not measure the success of your blog, it is still an essential component of any blog. After all, it will be the name that people will come to recognize and associate with your brand.

The most important thing to consider is your domain name should be easy to pronounce, spell, and memorize. The reason is for you to be able to share your blog more easily. For example, when someone asks for your blog at a party, you can just tell him the name of your blog without any need to clarify how to spell it properly, and you would not have to worry that he might forget about it. Therefore, avoid blog domain names that are long. The recommended length is one or two words. Three words can be used, but just be sure that it is not hard to memorize and understand. Also, avoid using a unique spelling for your blog; otherwise, you will have to explain the right spelling to everyone just for them to locate your site. It is best to keep your blog or domain name short and simple.

Customizing your blog

After opening an account with a reputable platform and choosing a host, you can now begin customizing your blog. Customization simply means designing your blog and arranging its layout and all its features. Designing your blog can take some time because there are endless ways to make your blog visually pleasing. The important thing is to ensure that your blog is presentable, and that it will be easy for your visitors to navigate your blog. Many blog platforms offer free templates. It is recommended that you use simple templates only. Using a template that has lots of bright colors and too many designs can make your blog look confusing and busy. If you do not like the free templates offered by your platform, you can also download free templates online, or you can also buy premium templates.

If you use WordPress, you might have to tweak some HTML code to further design our blog. The same goes for Blogger, but it may be simpler if you are using blogger. Take note, however, that a WordPress blog is more customizable than one on Blogger.

Add content to your blog

Once your blog is fully setup, you can now add your first blog post. Be careful with the content that you post on your blog. Be sure that every post is of good quality. A common mistake committed by many bloggers is first posting a few high-quality blog posts, and then following them with low-quality content. Always remember that it is better for you not to post any article or content at all than for you to have low-quality content on your blog.

After adding your first blog post, you can simply keep on adding high-quality content. How often you update your blog with new content varies. Some bloggers upload new posts daily, while others take some days before coming up with new content. The recommended approach is to update your blog with a new post at least once per week.

Before you upload any content, be sure to edit and proofread your work properly. Readers would not be happy to see grammar and punctuation errors in your article. A good habit to get into is to read your article several times before posting it. You should also read your article even after posting to be sure that there is nothing left for you to edit, and that the paragraph layout and article structure are properly observed once posted on your blog.

Designing Your Blog

The design of your blog is almost as important as the content posted to it. A well-designed blog tends to attract more readers and persuade them to stay and further explore the content. Here are some tips that you may consider when thinking about the design:

Be inspired

Look around you and observe your surroundings. Find out which colors or designs easily draw your attention. You can also browse online and get inspiration from the design of other blogs. From these inspirations, you can come up with your unique design that can better express what your blog is about.

Choose colors sensibly

Too many colors can be confusing; less is more. It is recommended that you stick to the following combination: any of the main primary colors and any color of your choice. You can also use gray to make the website look more professional. Note: With the right blog design, the use of contrasting colors can do wonders for your blog.

Goal-oriented

You should consider what your blog is about, and what you want it for. If your objective is to make your blog visitors buy something to generate sales, then you should have a well-written sales page on your blog. If your objective is to turn your visitors into subscribers, then your blog should have a direct email subscription or an attractive newsletter. To persuade your visitors to sign up, you should also make the signing-up process easy, fast, and convenient.

Conventional features

The conventional features are the common parts of a blog that people usually look for. If you want to give your visitors a better and complete blog experience, be sure to have these features on your blog:

- Headers

- Attribution to authors

- Pages

- Search bars

- Sidebars

- Options to subscribe

These features make navigating your blog easy and convenient for your visitors.

Images

As the old saying goes, "A picture is worth a thousand words", images really are so important in your blog. A blog with professional imagery scattered throughout is guaranteed to attract a higher viewership. I strongly recommend that you find sources of high quality images to use in your blogs, or if you know how, take the pictures yourself!

Think about the inent of the article. What are you trying to say? What image will draw the viewer in, and make them want to read more?

An excellent source of high quality imagery for use in blogs is www.shutterstock.com

Encourage interactions

One thing that makes a blog different from a traditional website is its level of interaction. Blogs usually have lots of engagement with its readers. Interacting with your visitors is also an effective way to establish a relationship with them, which is good when it comes to having regular traffic, as well as for increasing blog traffic. Therefore, be sure that there is a comment box on every post that you make, so people can easily interact with you. Keep the interactions flowing. Make sure to respond to your visitors in a timely manner, which will keep them coming back to your blog.

Responsive blog design

Since there are many ways to access the Internet these days, your blog should be responsive and look good on any device. Over 50% of all blog readers, now access their favourite blog through their mobile, so you must make sure that your blog looks great on a phone! This all comes down to the template that you use. A template, or website, that has been designed with all screen sizes in mind is known as "responsive". It responds to changes in screen size, changing it's layout, text and image sizing, to look great on smaller devices. Just as it can be viewed using a desktop computer, it should also be compatible when viewed using a tablet or mobile phone of different screen sizes. This will make your site easier to use and navigate, as well as increase the satisfaction of your visitors. Many of the pre-designed templates you can find on the well-known blogging platforms will be designed to be "responsive"...Make sure to pick one that is!

Experiment

There is no hard and fast rule for how to design the perfect blog. This is your opportunity to experiment with designs and layouts on your own. Be open to creative or unconventional ideas. Continue to find new ways to come up with a better blog. Experiment, learn and grow your blog.

Finding the Perfect Topic

Although there are numerous subjects to write about, our blog should not talk about different topics at random; otherwise, your visitors would not know what to expect or get from your blog. Therefore, you need to find a topic to specialize in — and this is why choosing a niche for your blog is so important. There are many niches to choose from, such as business, beauty, family, parenting, writing, travel, and spirituality, to name a few. The people that are interested in your niche are your target market. There are bloggers who take it a step further and narrow down the subject even more, for example, instead of just a general niche about parenting, they come up with a blog that is solely for parenting toddlers. Specialization is the key here. You will get more traffic and gain more followers with a specialty within a generalized niche that shows you know what you are talking about, as opposed to a Jack-of-All-Trades type of blogger.

For a beginner, it is suggested for you to focus on a single niche, so you will have fewer things to manage. After all, you can always grow into another niche at any time, either by including another niche in your already existing blog (as long as it fits within the same subject matter) or creating a brand-new blog for that subject. You are definitely free to manage more than one blog. In fact, many bloggers run several different blogs at the same time. Just be sure to establish yourself with one blog before branching out with more.

The question remains: How do you choose a profitable niche? It is worth noting that every niche can be profitable since there is always a market for any niche that you may choose. It is, however, strongly advised that you choose a niche or subject that you are personally interested in. This will allow you to enjoy writing about your interest, and your passion for it will come through to the reader. The reason is that blogging is a life-long journey. You also need to come up with fresh content on a regular basis. It is hard to have good content on your blog if you talk about something that you do not like or know little about. But, if it is something that you are passionate about, regardless of what it may be, you can always talk about it in an engaging and interesting manner — and this is important when you are blogging.

There are, of course, those who still become successful by having blogs that they themselves are not personally interested in. This is quite a challenge, especially for the beginner blogger. There is simply no sincerity in such blogs, except maybe a way to make money. Hence, always start with a subject that you love, a blog that you can spend writing hours or days without getting bored. It should be something that makes you happy. Although you can make money with your blog, you should realize that the main purpose of a blog is to share what you love or know with the world.

To get an idea as to the size of your niche, you should do a little research online using keywords that are related to your niche. If the search result pages return a good number of related articles, then it is a sign that there is a well-established market for your niche.

If your niche can be related to a product, for example, fashion and beauty, you can also make a search on Amazon using related keywords. If the result gives back a list of related products, then you know that there is a market for your niche. This also means there are other people who can promote your niche since there are products related to it that are being sold. Of course, those who sell such products also promote their products (or services) relevant to your chosen niche.

A pro tip would be to sign up to google keyword planner tool. Find it at http://adwords.google.com/KeywordPlanner. Once you have signed up, use the "Search for new keywords" section, and type in two or 3 keyword phrases related to the niche you have in mind.

You're going to want to find keywords that pull in a minimum of 1,000 global searches a month, but ideally, twice that amount. You'll also want to be sure that they are not overly competitive. Using this tool, can also be really valuable in finding out which sub niche you want to focus on.

For example, say that you had a general idea that you wanted to make a food blog, when searching for food blog recipes, you might find lots of other keywords related to that niche, which have a smaller (but still large), monthly search volume, which might direct the decision you make in choosing a sub niche.

It is also worth noting that getting a high number of results is not always a good sign since it can also signify tough competition.

To check how competitive a keyword is, simply go onto google.com, and type in you search phrase. So for example under "healthy breakfast recipes", we had a monthly search volume on keyword planner of 10 – 100k searches, which is very high. When typing it into google.com it found 71,800,000 results! Wow that's a lot of pages, and it probably means it will be very difficult for you to compete, and get ranked organically on the first couple of pages of google.

Now let's try something else – when searching the google keyword planner for "alkaline diet recipes" we still have a monthly search volume of 10 – 100k monthly searches, but guess what we now have only 2,000,000 results in google.com search.

You can see straight away that the second option has a similar amount of monthly traffic, but far less competition. This means it would be easier to rank on google for a blog built around the alkaline diet, than around healthy breakfasts.

This is just a simple example to get you thinking...There is really no hard and fast rules about what is "too competitive". My suggestion would be to brainstorm lots of sub niche ideas in your chosen niche, and put together a small spreadsheet of search volume, and total pages.

This should help you decide on the best opportunity for blogging, and for the overall direction of your blog.

Search Engine Optimization

Search engine optimization, or SEO, is a way to make our blog more visible on search engines. This leads to more traffic, which can also be converted into sales. After all, even if you have an excellent blog, there is no way you can make any profit out of it if people do not know that your blog even exists.

You should also consider the fact that there are many other blogs that are similar to yours. This is another part of the competition that demands your attention. Also, it should be noted that the creators of these blogs also work hard to be successful; therefore, you can be sure that they also exercise SEO strategies.

These days, SEO is a must to apply when you make a blog; otherwise, your blog will have low visibility, and will barely be detected by search engines. Now, there are many ways to increase your SEO ranking, but the most important part of any SEO strategy is the proper use of keywords — and this is something that you should learn and apply.

So, how do you use keywords to improve your blog's SEO ranking? The first step is to know the right keywords to use. You should use keywords on every new content or article that you post on your blog. When a person searches for something online, they will type something in the search bar of a favorite search engine. The words that they type are the keywords that you need to match. For example, if your blog is about natural living and health, you can write an article using the following keywords: home remedies for a fever. Now, this will increase the chances of your blog of being found should anyone look online for home remedies to cure a fever. The closer your keywords match those that people will type in the search bar, the better your chances of being found.

On-Page Optimization

Be sure to fill EVERY section on the backend of your blog properly. For example fill in all Titles, Meta Tags, Descriptions, Alt Tags for images, etc. Use consistent and proper formatting for headlines, bullets, and descriptions.

Filling in all of these fully, and with keyword rich descriptions, will work wonders for your SEO ranking.....don't be lazy! Take the time to get this right.

Long-tail keywords

A long time ago, one or two keywords were enough to enhance visibility. However, today, with so many blogs and websites out there, you need to use a keyword phrase, or what experts call long-tail keywords. This means that you should avoid using generic keywords. For example, do not just use the keywords, Steve Jobs, if you have an article about him. Instead, aim for a longer keyword phrase, such as "Steve Jobs's rules for success". By doing so, there will be greater chances of your blog being found should people look for Steve Jobs's rules to become successful. A pro tip would be to use the keyword planner tool, when researching new blog content ideas. Try to inject valuable keyword phrases throughout your blog content. Over time google will start to see you blog as an authority on your particular niche, and rank you accordingly.

Keyword density

Do remember that the use of keywords alone is not enough. Merely filling in your article with tons of keywords will, in fact, cause it to not rank high in search engines. The suggested practice is to follow a keyword density of around 1%-3%. This means that for every 100 words, you should aim to repeat your keywords only once, twice, or three times at the most.

Backlinks

Another critical part of ranking on search engines, is the proper use of backlinks. What is a backlink you say? Any link from one webpage to one of your blog articles is a backlink.

I strongly recommend that you link between your own blog articles, wherever appropriate. This is not only good for SEO purposes, but it also means your readers are more likely to be able to find great content on your site to continue reading.

You can also reach out to other bloggers & niche related websites, to feature you blog, or to share you blog posts with their audience.

Over time, if you diligently work to create VALUABLE backlinks, and appropriately keyword RICH blog articles, you will see more and more organic traffic coming to your site from google, and other search engines. Do not keyword stuff....google actually penalizes websites for this. Also make sure that your backlinks are high quality links, from trusted reliable sources. Do not pay for a "backlink service", as this will harm your website authority.

Content Creation

Every successful blog depends on the content that you produce. If your blog has excellent content and you put in a good amount of effort to promote it, then chances will be that you can have a successful blogging career. However, let us admit the fact that it is not easy to come up with high-quality content often. It is not uncommon to find blogs that have about 30% good-quality content, but then suffer from 70% low-quality postings. Remember the rule: Never post anything that is of poor quality.

Now, how do you create meaningful content on your blog? Generally, you have two choices: either you write the content yourself or ask someone else to do it for you. If you write the content yourself, it may be because you have the expertise and knowledge on the subject of your blog or, if you are not familiar with the subject, you can do the research on your own. Of course, the best way is still for you to write what you know best. Therefore, as already mentioned, it is well advised that you make a blog on something that you are passionate about or at least interested in.

Get inspired! Read other blog articles in you niche for new content ideas. Take inspiration from books, magazines, your home or your work space. I actually love to take a small note book with me wherever I go, so that when inspiration strikes, I can copy my idea down for later reference.

The world really is you oyster. Train yourself to see the world through the view of finding inspiration for your blog, and you will be surprised with what you come up with.

If you struggle for time, inspiration, or skill, you can, of course, ask for the help of another to create the contents of your blog. You can do this by hiring a ghostwriter. A ghostwriter is a person you can hire to write the entries for you for a fee. The ghostwriter will not have any ownership over the work. This means that you are considered to be the author of the work that your ghostwriter creates. Normally, there is a non-disclosure agreement between the ghostwriter and the one who contracts (you) a ghostwriter to the effect that the project will remain a secret between you and them (the ghostwriter).

Although legal, there are some ethical issues that arise when people hire ghostwriters. Some say that it is fraudulent because you get to claim ownership as an author of something that you have not written yourself. Others say that it is an example of misrepresentation. However, in practice, hiring a ghostwriter is normal and is widely used, even by professional writers. Sometimes the bulk of writing assignments becomes too hard to manage, so many writers hire ghostwriters to do the job for them. Others simply have no time to write and rely on the expertise of a ghostwriter.

Still, the best and most professional way to hire a ghostwriter is to tell your ghostwriter what you want to be written. By doing so, you can rightfully claim ownership of the work without any issue, since the finished product (your article or book) is full of your own ideas and not just views and opinions coming from your ghostwriter. This is actually the proper way people hire ghostwriters. They merely convert your thought and ideas into words. Unfortunately, many people these days abuse the services of a ghostwriter by simply telling the ghostwriter the topic of the article or book, and the ghostwriter is the one who does the research and writes their own ideas and understanding of the subject.

Where to find a ghostwriter

There are many places where you can find and hire a ghostwriter. By simply doing a search online, you will find many ghostwriters who will offer you their services for a fee. If you want to find cheap ghostwriters, you can try content mills, such as Freelancer, Guru, and Upwork. The problem here is that most, if not all, of the writers from these content mills, have low-quality work. Since they will be paid fee is quite low, they tend to write so fast with little focus on the quality of their work.

If you want, you can also try Fiverr. Fiverr is a place online where people post different kinds of gigs or services that they offer to the public. You can find writers there who will write an article for you for at least $5 (hence the name, Fiverr). However, just like with content mills, be cautious of the writers that you will meet on this site since you cannot expect high-quality work for just $5. Good writers know that they deserve a nice pay and usually look for writing clients elsewhere.

If you do plan to write them yourself but feel unsure about how engaging you are as a writer, you can always hire an editor. They can check your article and give feedback on what to improve. You will still have control over your content, but having an editor will guide you in the right direction.

In conclusion, the most recommended way is for you to come up with your own articles and write them. After all, your blog should be your personal space. It is best if you take full control of everything. It is not a requirement to be a professional writer to run a blog. What is important is the value that you share, and the information that your readers can get by visiting your site. With just a few months or weeks of writing, you can improve the quality of your skills to a decent level.

Just start writing, and you will find over time, that you see great improvements in your writing style!

Blog vs. Website

Some people are concerned about the difference between a blog and a website. It is safe to say that there is almost no difference between the two since a blog is also a website. However, for the word geeks out there, you can spot some distinguishing differences. For one, a blog is more active than a website. A blog gets regular updates; you can see new posts on a blog usually on a weekly basis, while such updates do not usually happen on a website. The level of interaction is also much higher on a blog, while there is almost no interaction with a website. The only interaction within a website might be through the Contact Us page. In a way, a website is more formal than a blog. A blog is like Facebook or other social media but there is no limit to how much content or characters you can write or post. You can try to compare the blog of Paulo Coelho with the website of Apple to see these glaring differences.

*Note: This book uses the words website and blog synonymously.

Chapter 2: Making Money with Your Blog

The money that you can earn with your blog is one of the reasons why some people take blogging seriously. In fact, even those who have no interest in writing or sharing their thoughts, sometimes delve into blogging to see just how profitable it can be for them. It is important to point out that most (if not all) of the successful blogs out there are written by bloggers who are truly passionate about their topic and do not just come up with contents just for the sake of earning money.

Now, with your blog design ready, and hopefully enjoying some nice traffic, here are some effective ways to make money with your blog:

Sell a product or service

Normally, bloggers write about topics that they really know. You can sell a product on your blog to earn a nice profit. Bloggers often sell e-books on their blog. Instead of a product, you can offer a service. For example, if your blog is about the English language, you can offer a tutorial service on your blog, which will allow you to teach your blog visitors English on a more personal level. You can also offer other services, such as writing services, consulting services, and so on. Take note that the Internet is full of consumers, as long as you have something to offer, there is sure to be a market for it. Always remember that you have the whole world as your potential market for your product or service.

Really try to understand who it is that is visiting our blog. What is it that is driving them? What is their need or their desire? Can you satisfy that need or desire through a paid product or service?

A word of caution though...Blog readers don't want to be bombarded with your sales pitch. It's really important that you nurture your customer relationship. They must feel that you are MOST interested in helping them, providing them with useful free content, and interacting with them. THEN from that place of relationship and trust, find a way to market your product or service from them.

Make all of your useful, free content most prominent on your blog, otherwise it will just come across as a sales pitch website, which is a massive turn off for your readers. Nurture your customer relationship.

We really recommend setting up an email capture somewhere on your website so that you can start to build an email list. Provide your email list with real value. Give them great content. Build their trust. Once you have got their trust, you can start to market products or services from them easily and naturally.

Affiliate marketing

Another effective way that bloggers make handsome profits from their blog is by affiliate marketing. This is where you promote the products and services of other people or companies on your blog. You can earn a profit each time a person clicks on the affiliate link you provide, and you can get more profit each time a visitor makes a purchase through your link. Many bloggers make thousands of dollars a month just by affiliate marketing. The usual rate of commission is about 10% up to 30% of the sale price. So, just imagine how much you can earn. Make sure you have adequate traffic to your blog before starting with affiliated links.

To do affiliate marketing, you need to join an affiliate program. You should sell a product or service that you truly believe is helpful to people. It is hard to recommend something that you do not believe in. Do not forget to put a disclaimer each time you promote a product in order to avoid some legal liability, such as "This article contains affiliated links". Of course, you can still promote those things that you yourself have not yet tried or even those that you do not personally believe in. However, again, it is hard to convince people to buy a product if you are not convinced yourself that the product is a good one. You want to build trust with your audience, and this will help you in earn money from affiliated products. Your audience trusts your recommendations.

You can try joining well-established affiliate marketing programs, such as Amazon Associates and Clickbank. There are many people who earn a full-time income simply by focusing on affiliate marketing. Just be careful because even though there are experts who claim to make a huge amount of income per month through affiliate marketing, many of these "experts" are hacks and scams. This means that they are lying and simply want to promote themselves as an "expert" even if they have sold only a few affiliate products or services.

Pay-per-click advertising

Pay-per-click ads, or PPC, is another popular way to earn from your blog. When you do PPC, ads are posted on your blog. You get paid per view, or per click, or even per sale that is made, depending on the contract. There are many providers that you can find online that offer this kind of program, such as Clicksor and Chitika. However, the most famous PPC program is still Google Adsense or simply Adsense. Adsense has the highest return when compared to other PPC programs.

Joining a PPC program is also free and easy. Normally, you just have to sign up for an account and choose the ads that you want to display on your blog. You then earn money based on the agreement that you have. The more traffic that you bring into your blog, the more chances that you will earn bigger profits.

Again...another word of warning here. Choose your display ads very carefully. Make sure they are related to your niche, and that they are services or products that you really believe in, and that you believe your customers would really love to have. Make sure they are attractive and positioned nicely. Don't sell out! There's nothing more off-putting than a website full of random advertising, with no real relevance to the niche or site. Think of your customer, and that customer relationship. What would you want to see on a blog that you where reading?

Cost-per-mile advertising

Cost-per-mile advertising, or CPM, is similar to PPC. However, instead of being paid per click, you get paid based on the number of impressions or page views that you get. Normally, you get a fixed amount per 1,000 views. You can fund many services online that offer CPM. If your blog has lots of traffic, then CPM may be the best way to monetize your blog.

Advertising widget

This is similar to PPC. However, to make it simpler to place ads on your blog, you only have to upload a widget. The way you are paid with an advertising widget depends on the time that you have it on your site. Usually, you both fix a time as to how long you will display the widget on your blog, you then get paid a certain sum of money regardless of how many people click on the advertising widget. Some advertisers will offer you an additional fee per click in addition to the fixed amount for having the widget on your blog.

Tutorial

You can get more personal and offer tutorial services on your blog. For example, if your blog is about books, you can offer a writing tutorial to your blog visitors for a fee. It depends on you if you want it to be on a per class or per hour basis. There are also many ways to teach your students. A common way to do this is via Skype where you can video chat and talk as if you were actually together in real time. If you have video editing capabilities, you can create Youtube videos for only those who subscribe to your tutorials.

What about workbooks, or ebooks, showing how to do a specific task related to your niche? Can you teach your reader something that that want?

You might be surprised at how many things you could impart to your reader in a paid tutorial, or service.

Courses

Many bloggers offer courses on their blog. A person may enroll in a course, and there is a syllabus to be followed. You can also add an exam at the end of a syllabus to test how much a student has learned. These courses can be of different topics, but they should be something that you are an expert at. You can divide a subject into mini-courses, so you can have many courses to offer. Be sure to make the prices reasonable, and the courses should be professionally made. You do not want the people who take your course to feel like they have been fooled by you or that the course was less than worth the money that they spent. It is good to offer tutorial and courses once you establish yourself as an expert in your niche.

You can either sell your course for a fixed price (great for email marketing), or you can use the subscription model, where your reader signs up to be a member of your site, paying a small monthly fee, in order to access lots of additional content, or course material on your site.

If you go the subscription route, this can be an amazing source of income.

Having 100 people sign up to a $20/ month subscription is an easy way to completely replace your income! Bear in mind that you will need to provide significant, ongoing value to the customer. What would you be willing to pay for the course content you are planning to create? Would you still be satisfied after 2-3 months or would you be likely to cancel your subscription?

Certainly, the subscription model has amazing potential to make A LOT of money, but it takes A LOT of work.

Sponsored posts

Once you establish a good following, you can also earn money through sponsored posts on your site. This involves reviewing a product. You can get products to review from BlogPRWire, Tomoson, SheSpeaks, and other similar sites. Take note that you should be careful with the products that you choose to review. It is best to be as honest as possible, and only promote those that are worthy of being promoted. If you do not know the product personally, try to find out as much as you can about the product. You can try searching for reviews made by buyers on Amazon and other websites. Also, do not just review any product. It should be included in, or at least related to, your chosen niche. Otherwise, your blog visitors may not take any interest in your review. Try you best to provide real value to your reader, but choosing products that you really believe in.

Join Fiverr

Fiverr is a place where you can offer gigs. If you have a blog that has a huge following, then you can probably make lots of money with Fiverr. Different kinds of gigs are offered at Fiverr at the price of $5 (minimum). Many sellers on Fiverr earn money just by sharing stuff on their blog. For example, an author may contact you to help promote his book by posting it (and a link to the book) on your blog. Many sellers on Fiverr earn thousands of dollars just by doing this. If you are interested in this, I suggest that you get started by setting yourself up with an account on fiverr. Create some basic gigs related to "guest entry blog posts" or "product review blog" etc.

Paid membership

You can have some parts of your site only accessible with a membership. To be a member, visitors will need to pay a certain fee. To persuade people to pay and be a member, the free stuff on your site should be informative and helpful; otherwise, your blog visitors will think that the private or locked area only for paid members probably offers just the same simple, free contents. Also, you do not want to make your site only useful for paid members. Therefore, do not forget to update your free stuff. A good way to do this is to release a part of the paid features of the blog little by little, while you continue to add more materials to the private or paid area of the blog.

Sell your blog

This is a way to make tons of money. You can try Flippa or other platforms where you can offer your blog for sale. A good blog that generates regular traffic usually sells for thousands of dollars. But, of course, this also means saying goodbye to your blog. Do take note that you can always come up with another blog. In fact, you can also manage more than one blog at the same time. If you find that your interest in the topic of the blog is waning or you find it difficult to come up with meaningful content, selling your blog is always an option.

How much you can sell your blog for depends on how valuable you honestly think it is. Do not forget the hours of labor that you put into your blog, as well as any expenses with promotion, hiring ghostwriters/editors, and so on. Selling a successful blog is where making a large amount of money is possible; however, the drawback is also high since you will completely lose your blog and all connections to it. You may or may not choose to take this approach. After all, it is not uncommon to find bloggers who grow very attached to their blogs.

Chapter 3: Grow Your Blog

This chapter will teach you how to effectively grow your blog into a prospering business. This is about making your blog draw a high amount of traffic. As you may already know, the more traffic to your blog attracts will usually equal more profit for you.

Take advantage of social media

If you want your content to go viral on the Internet, then you need to tap the power of social media. In fact, social media is the key to getting regular visitors to your blog, especially for newcomers. There are many social media platforms to choose from, such as Facebook, Twitter, LinkedIn, and GooglePlus, to name a few. The two most popular platforms among these are Facebook and Twitter. Therefore, make sure that you promote your blog on these channels. If you are not a fan of using social media, you can just use one channel (either Facebook or Twitter) but be sure to take advantage of social media regardless. If you are adamant about not engaging in social media, and if you are using Blogger as your blogging platform, then you can simply use GooglePlus to automatically promote your posts. Join a relevant community in your niche, add some interesting people, and have your posts automatically posted to GooglePlus. By doing so, you will have automatic viewers each time you upload a new post on your blog. Of course, the more you grow your circle, the more readers you will have. This means a bigger market reach, which means more potential profits for your business.

Please note that you should avoid the practice of abusing the use of social media to promote your blog. If you continuously bombard your followers or connections with promotions, they might start to think that you are only spamming them and you might lose your followers before you even realize it. The hard part here is that once you lose your connections, it will be almost impossible to convince them to connect with you again. Hence, take care in crafting and maintaining your image. You should promote your blog professionally without sounding as if you are begging for page views or visitors.

E-mail list

Make sure that your blog has a subscription button, so people can subscribe and join your email list. This will allow them to get a notification sent to their email each time you post something new on your blog. Of course, to convince people to sign up to your email list, they must first like the contents of your blog enough to want to come back. Therefore, be sure to fill your blog with useful and high-quality information.

Newsletter

First, let us be clear about one thing: There is a difference between e-mail marketing and a newsletter. In essence, they are the same in the sense that a subscriber will receive something new from your blog. However, the difference lies in the contents of a newsletter and the contents of your subscriber in the case of email marketing.

On the one hand, in regards to a newsletter, it should function as a traditional newspaper with valuable, free content. It can also contain sales promotions, but such promotions should be kept to a minimum since the purpose of a newsletter, just like a newspaper, is to inform and not to offer something for sale. E-mail marketing focuses more on promotional emails and may or may not offer any free content. The frequency of these two marketing tools differs also. Newsletters are usually sent on a regular basis, while email marketing is done sporadically. After all, no subscriber would want to receive sales offers regularly. You also do not want to bombard your subscribers' inbox with sales offers since they might feel that you only want to make money from them. When running a blog, it is also important to carefully craft the brand image that you want to project to your visitors and subscribers.

Guest posting

A good way to promote your blog is to guest post on another blog that is in the same niche as yours. There are many blogs online that accept guest posts. In fact, some of them will even pay you to post on their site. Hence, you will not only get paid, but you can also get some promotion at the same time. Many of these blogs are well-established sites. Therefore, it is almost guaranteed that they will bring new and significant traffic to your blog.

The challenge with guest posting is that the owner or manager of the site where you want to guest post must like your manuscript. Hence, this usually takes some well-versed writing skills. If your writing is not subpar, then you can hire a professional ghostwriter to come up with a good article for you.

Most blogs that accept guest postings post on their blog that they are open to such content. Another sign that a blog accepts guest posts is if the blog has many authors. Also, it does not hurt to politely ask the owner of a blog if you can guest post on his blog. You can do this by sending a message to the site's administrator. You can usually find a way to connect with the administrator by clicking on the Contact Us page of a site, or any page that will allow you to send a message. Reputable sites usually have a page on how you can contact the blog owner. You can also connect using social media. Again, this is another advantage of being present on social media. Being on social media can guarantee a connection with guest posting blogs.

Most blogs that accept guest posting will allow you to write a short bio of yourself and even a link to your site. This is your chance to promote your blog to a high number of readers. Make sure you have something of great value to offer to their readers.

Participate in online forums

Whatever the subject of your niche, chances are there are online forums about the same subject. You can take advantage of this by participating in such forums. You can identify an active forum by checking the latest dates of the posts in a particular forum. Just like when commenting in social media, remember to observe professionalism and decency. Feel free to drop a short line to promote your blog. Be sure to become an active member of the forum and not just there to post about your blog, to never be heard from again.

Use Fiverr

There are people on Fiverr who are willing to promote your blog for just $5. However, just a word of caution: Be careful of buying services on Fiverr that says they will drive thousands and thousands in traffic to your blog, even if they claim that the traffic will come from social media. The reason is that such visitors are not real people, but are mostly bots. Therefore, even though you can get lots of visits, there is no way you can convert them into money. Also, there is a risk that Google might suspend the ads posted on your blog because such activity can be considered as cheating. When you use Fiverr, remember the saying that when it sounds too good to be true, it probably is. Good gigs to get on Fiverr for promotion include those that will post your blog on their blog, as well as those who will post your blog on social media. Keep in mind that no seller can guarantee any sales conversion.

Chapter 4: Advanced Tips and Tricks

In order to steadily increase your rate of success, you need to observe the best practices applied by the top bloggers. These practices can help you generate a consistent flow of readership, as well as increased sales numbers.

Do not rewrite other articles

Many bloggers these days have the bad habit of simply rewriting the contents of another blog. This is not only unprofessional, but it can also hold you liable for plagiarism. After all, plagiarism is not just about failing to cite your source but also covers things where a person claims to be the author of an idea that belongs to someone else. Therefore, even if the new rewritten content cannot be detected by Copyscape Premium or any other plagiarism checking website, it does not always mean that it is already free from plagiarism. Any readers from the original blog that happen by your's may sense that your article is strangely familiar, and notify the original author.

Fill in the gaps within your niche

There are many ways to approach the same subject. Just because many articles have already been written about a particular topic does not mean that you can no longer write a unique and engaging article for it. All that you need to do is view the subject from a different perspective. For example, instead of writing an article about the health benefits of drinking tea, you can come up with an article about the bad effects of drinking black tea for teenagers. By approaching a subject differently and being more specific, you can come up with a unique touch to the same subject matter. Filling in such gaps in your niche or covering something that has not yet been covered by other articles online, and in print, can be a goldmine for bloggers, especially when the post becomes viral on social media.

Be sure to properly research for the article so as to keep misinformation from spread on the internet.

Let an influencer promote your blog

Influencers are those people who have a strong influence and huge followers with respect to a particular topic. Just imagine if the influencer is the one who promotes your blog? The next time you publish a new article on your blog, why not reach out to an influencer in your niche and ask for some help? You can use BuzzStream to identify and connect with big influencers. Simply fill in the information on a particular niche using keywords, and you will get a list of contact information of people that belong to your chosen niche. You can then send them a message to ask for a quote and ways on how you can work together. Of course, there is no guarantee that an influencer will help you, but there is a chance that he might like your article and even help you promote it, and your blog.

This is where having a professional-looking blog is going to increase your success of connecting to influencers. The article you are pitching to an influencer needs to be of high quality with well-researched information.

Use LinkedIn to get connected with influencers

Here is a secret: You can use LinkedIn to connect with influencers also. Many influencers have a LinkedIn account, and you can more easily connect with them on LinkedIn, especially if you are a connection in the 2nd degree area. Once you are connected, you can then send a message to the inbox of your chosen influencers.

Correct grammar

It is disappointing to read an informative article that is full of grammatical errors. It may be difficult to come up with lots of content that is free of any grammar mistakes, but at least strive to have as few mistakes as possible. You do not need to be an English major to have a successful blog. However, this does not mean that you can write any way you want and still expect to have a regular flow of readership. You should, at least, observe the basic rules of grammar. If grammar is not your strong point, a good tip to follow is simply to stick to basic tenses. Also, you may use the grammar correction feature (if any is available) of your favorite writing application, but do not rely on it completely. Some mistakes in grammar cannot be detected even by the most advanced grammar check application or feature. Therefore, it is highly recommended that you read your article several times before (and even after) you publish it.

If your application does not have a spell/grammar check feature, you can always use Grammarly.com to check for grammatical issues in your work.

Call to action

If you are selling something on your site or if you need visitors to do something specific, you should include a call to action. A call to action tells your reader what to do next. It can be as simple as reading another article on your blog or telling him to sign up on your e-mail list. It is well advised to place a call to action at the bottom of your post. It should be the last message that your visitor gets to read when he reads an article. Also, keep your call to action short, direct, and clear.

It is worth noting that people who surf the web in search of answers are most likely to accept a suggestion. The fact that they are willing to listen to other people's ideas on the net means that they are open to suggestions. This is something that you can take advantage of. Of course, no matter what you do, you cannot have someone follow your call to action if it is obvious that you are only trying to fool them. Therefore, make sure that your call to action is practical, realistic, and believable. Last but not least, the contents of your blog should be helpful to the reader.

Establish trust

If there is one thing that is common among successful bloggers, it is the presence of trust. People trust their blogs. But, how do you establish this trust? For starters, you should always come up with helpful and informative content. Having regular interactions with your blog visitors is also a good way to establish trust. Also, when you cite a source, make sure that you direct a link to a reputable site. For example, if you cite a source on a topic that is related to health, do not just link to another blog or site that talks about health. Instead, link to a well-established and credible site such as Mayo Clinic.

Do not buy followers

It is impressive to see bloggers who have a huge number of followers or connections. This is true, especially if their blog has many real engagements. Now, when you surf the net, it is not uncommon to find a service that will give you thousands of followers in exchange for a few bucks. In essence, you simply have to buy followers. While this may seem enticing, the point here is that you should not buy any followers. Just the fact that you are buying followers for your blog is unethical practice. The next reason is that such services will only send you fake followers, or followers that are not real humans. They are made of bots or fake accounts not actually used by a real human being. The problem here is that you can end up with a blog that boasts a very high number of followers but has little or no engagements. This will only make it obvious that you only bought your followers or connections, which is not something you want connected to you or your brand image.

Instead of wasting your money on buying followers, use your money and efforts to create better content. Followers automatically come once you fill your blog with high-quality information. Remember, the value of a blog is not measured by the number of followers that it has, but by the quality of articles or contents posted there. After all, the true essence of blogging is still about sharing and expressing yourself, and not about gaining followers.

Avoid keyword stuffing

Keyword stuffing is the practice of stuffing your article with lots of keywords or using the same keywords so many times in the same article. Unfortunately, some people still think that the use of keywords is the only thing that matters when it comes to increasing visibility on search engines. However, this is not the case.

Long ago, stuffing your article with keywords was effective, but then Google and other search engines realized this practice and have since improved how their search engines rank websites. Today, if you stuff your article with keywords, it will cause a drop instead of an increase in SEO ranking. The quality of your article matters a lot. Stuffing your article with keywords will result in low-quality content, which is not good for SEO, or any other purpose. This is why producing high-quality contents cannot be overemphasized because it is very important.

Use images

As they say, a picture speaks a thousand words. It is good practice to use images, even just a single image, per post. Visiting a blog that is full of nothing but plain text can be very intimidating and boring.

Of course, each image that you use should be related to the contents of your article or post. Be aware that you cannot use all the images that you find online for your blog. For starters, you can only use those images that are part of the public domain, or you can simply take the picture yourself. In all other cases, you need to ask the permission of the original source (image designer, artist, photographer, etc.), and he must give his consent.

Public domain images are those images that can be used by anyone even without permission. You can find many images of this kind online by including the keyword phrase "public domain images" in the search bar. You can also filter Google's search result pages to display only images of public domains. But, to make sure that you use a completely unique image or photo on your blog, you can simply take the picture yourself. Blog photos do not have to be perfect, but they must be appealing, or at least entertaining, to the reader.

As mentioned earlier, I strongly suggest that you purchase your stock media for your blog, through websites like shutterstock.com. These come with a license enabling you to post it on your blog without any copyright issues.

Add ALT texts to images

While adding images to your posts is good practice, simply adding images alone will not make your blog more discoverable in search engines. If you want your images to help make your site more visible, you should add ALT texts to every image that you have on your blog. Without using ALT texts, search engines will not be able to recognize what the image is. Take note that search engines need text to be able to understand a particular image. ALT test is simply a short description that you usually see below an image.

High Quality

Make sure every post you make is of high quality. Having high-quality content is the key to a successful blog. You may be asking yourself, what is a high-quality content? The first thing that you should know about providing high-quality content is that it should be informative. Your blog visitor must be able to get the information or knowledge that he needs pertaining to a specific subject. Unfortunately, some blog posts have excellent titles, but the content of the article lacks enough information to satisfy a curious reader. There are two ways you can get the information that you can write on your blog: it can come from your own experience and knowledge, and/or from research. Take note not to forget to cite your sources, if any.

It is also worth noting that coming up with an informative article is not always enough. Another important thing that you need is to be able to express this information clearly in writing. You do not need to be a professional writer to maintain a successful blog, but you do need to develop some basic writing skills. If you are the type of person who can effectively express your thoughts and ideas in words, then this should not be a problem.

Pay attention to the flow of your article. The way to do this is to read the article out loud. If you notice anything strange with the flow of the words, then do not hesitate to edit your work. If the lines do not flow naturally, then you need to make some adjustments, perhaps add a few more words or remove some. This entirely depends on how the article is written. It is also good practice to ask someone to read your work before you publish it. However, this option is not always available. What you can do is to delay publishing your work. Do not look at your manuscript for a whole day, and then read it again with a fresh mind the next day.

Citing your sources is also important for two reasons: to avoid plagiarism and to increase the credulity of your posts. There are many ways to cite a source. You can follow the APA style or even Chicago style of citing sources. You can find guides on how to cite sources online. If you find these guides confusing, you can simply cite the source any way that you want, just be sure to cite the name of your source, and even a link to the website you retrieved it from.

Good design and layout

Your blog's design and layout are important key components of your blog. When you search for templates that you can use, you can be tempted to use a template that features bright colors and exquisite designs. Although it can be very tempting to use such designs, it is strongly recommended that you stick to a template that is simplistic. Having busy designs can make your blog look complicated to navigate and, sometimes, it can decrease the readability of your contents. Remember that your blog's design should work to highlight the contents of your blog and not the other way around. The use of black, white, or gray, is also suggested to enhance the professional look of the blog.

The layout of your blog is also important. Your blog's layout should make it easy for your visitors to navigate. It should also highlight the important parts of your blog. Everything should be organized. Just like with the design of your blog, a simple layout is also suggested. The reason why you make it simple is so that it will be easy for your visitors to use, understand, and navigate.

Use white spaces

Use white spaces. But, if white is not the color of your background, then use your background's primary color instead of white. The thing to remember is to utilize the use of space. Have you been to a house that is so cramped because of the amount of clutter inside the house? The same applies to your blog. Do not fill your entire blog with posts. Be sure to use spaces. Having spaces can make your blog look cleaner.

Spaces also separate one part of a blog from the others, which is good for easier navigation. However, you should not over-do the use of spaces. Keep in mind that your visitors read your blog not because of the spaces which do not give them any new information, but because of the contents of your blog. Be sure to use them wisely.

Promote on social media

An excellent way to draw traffic to your blog is by promoting it on social media. As already mentioned, Facebook and Twitter are two of the most common social media platforms that you can use, among many others.

Of course, the use of social media alone is not enough. You still need to come up with high-quality content. You also need to build a good following. The more active followers you have, then all the more potential traffic you can generate. Take note that we are talking about active followers. They are your followers or friends online who connect with you and are truly interested in your posts. They usually demonstrate such interest by commenting or sharing your posts with their own network.

The key to the use of social media is to promote other people. As you may notice, the way that social media works is to treat others the way you would like to be treated. If you keep on liking and re-sharing content of other people, you can expect them to treat you in the same manner. However, if you only focus on promoting yourself, you may not have a good number of engagements on social media, subject to a few exceptional cases (Example: celebrities).

Engage with other people's contents

If you want people to take a chance to look at your blog and make a reaction, you should also engage with their posts. Again, in social media, you can expect to get the same treatment just like the way you treat others. When you write a comment, be mindful of your language. Never use offensive words. It is better for you not to place a comment instead of reacting in a negative way. Also, do not comment just for the sake of commenting. Be sure to be honest and sincere with your comments and responses.

Use Google Keyword Planner

As mentioned in the first chapter, you need to use keywords to increase your SEO ranking. The higher your SEO ranking, the more visible your blog is in the Internet world. However, you can only come up with so many keywords. How do you know which ones are good enough? You can use Google Keyword Planner. This tool is completely free to use. To use this feature from Google, you first need to sign up for Google Adwords. Adwords is Google's program that will allow you to create Google Ads to promote your blog. Sign-up for Adwords is also free. Once you have an Adwords account, you can now access and use Google Keyword Planner.

When you use Google Keyword Planner, you will be able to know the number of hits of certain keyword phrases. You will also get suggestions from Google about other keywords that you can use. By doing so, you will know which keywords are regularly being searched, how many searches are made pertaining to specific keyword phrases, as well as the location of the people who do those searches using Google's search engine. This will allow you to have a better strategy as to what keywords to use.

Use Google Adwords

Google Adwords will allow you to create ads that will appear each time a person searches your chosen keywords. These are paid ads. The good news is that you can control how much you are willing to pay. One of the best things about Google Adwords is that you only get charged each time someone clicks on your ads. Hence, you always get your money's worth. You can also control the territory where you want your ads to appear. If you want, you can have your ads only to appear in the U.S. or specific states in the U.S. Using Google Adwords is also a good way to increase you SEO since other people can visit your blog through your ads. It is a god idea to use Adsense if you offer something for sale on your blog. However, the drawback is that you might have to spend a lot of money if you just want to rely on Adsense to draw traffic to your blog. Also, when you use Adsense, it is advised that you should already have a complete blog that has lots of useful content. If you only have a new blog with few contents, then there is nothing much to get from your blog. Your objective is first to give your blog a good foundation by filling it with useful and helpful contents to attract visitors.

There is one common issue about using Adsense, and that is many people do not get approved to display Google ads on their blog. It is worth noting that your account must first be approved by Google before it can display Google ads. The challenge is that not all people get their accounts approved. So, is it really that difficult to make your account eligible to display Google ads? The answer to this question is yes, if you know the right approach to take to get approved. So, what is the right approach that will persuade Google to grant your account permission to display ads? Well, there are some things that you need to consider:

- Make sure that your blog already has a good number of posts. Google will not allow your blog to display ads if you only have a few posts. There is no rule as to the minimum number of posts that you should have, but you should aim to have at least 30 good-quality posts.

- Your blog should already have a regular stream of readership. And, no, you do not need to have a high amount of traffic. However, you do need to have a regular flow of traffic.

- Join GooglePlus. Okay, this one is not a requirement but is very helpful. Now, when you join GooglePlus, you should also join the communities that are related to your blog. Come to think of it, how can Google deny you access to ads if you promote your blog using its own product, GooglePlus? By joining GooglePlus and being active on the platform will also guarantee you a good amount of blog visitors. This is true, especially when you participate in the communities that are related to your blog. Of course, simply joining GooglePlus alone is not enough; you still need to show Google that your blog is worthy of displaying ads. Although there is no certainty of being accepted, GooglePlus can significantly increase your chances of being granted the benefit of displaying Google ads.

Write compelling comments

Remember those blogs that have a huge number of followers? How would you feel if you can drive those followers to your blog? The good news is that all that you need to do is to write about three to five sentences of a compelling commentary. The way to do this is to spot a well-established blog that has an active post. This refers to posts with lots of engagements from other people. You then write your own compelling comment and draw the attention of everyone. Now, there are two ways to write a compelling comment: You can raise an issue which usually contradicts the original post, or you can praise the post and add something new in a way that will spark the interest of others.

The first way is rather risky because you might fail to convince other people to follow you. Should you decide to raise an issue, be sure to express it in a respectful manner and always have a good basis to support your argument. The second way is what is recommended since you do not have to go against the writing of the original post on another person's blog. This is also a good way to establish a relationship with other bloggers. The key here is to improve the flow of your writings, as well as your choice of words. Instead of simply saying that a particular post is nice and informative, write about what makes it nice and informative. Highlight the lines that drew your attention, and then add your own positive twist on the subject. Usually, when people read this kind of comment, they try to know more about the one who wrote the comment. Of course, you can lead them to your site once they click your profile image which can appear when you comment, or you can discreetly leave a link to your blog after your commentary. Of course, only praise a blog post if it is really worth praising; otherwise, people can easily tell that you are merely trying to sound good to draw traffic to your blog.

Be Cordial

A sound piece of advice often given to lawyers is to always be a cordial, even in the face of a harsh adversary. The same advice should be followed by bloggers. It is almost inevitable that you will experience negative comments from time to time. Do not let such comments discourage you. Instead, try to see if the comments hold water. If justifiable, then make adjustments in the development of your blog. However, if the comments were made simply for the purpose of saying something bad without good reason, then reply to the comment politely and professionally. Failing that, just ignore them!

Timing

Timing is important in business, and blogging is no different. You should observe proper timing when you post something new on your blog. The best time to update your blog with a new post is the time when your connections or followers are also available online. Now, there is no hard and fast rule as to when is the best time to post something new on your blog. Since your connections will be spread across the world, the right time varies depending on your location as well as the Internet habits of your connections.

You can find out the best time to post new content through trial and error. Simply post at different times of the day, and find out which post receives the best number of responses. You can then determine the best time for you to upload a new post. Take note that since your connections will continue to grow, the best time for you to share a new post may also change in the near future. Be sure to continue experimenting to get the best result as your base grows.

Use sharing buttons

Make sure that your posts are easy to share. Ideally, a visitor should be able to share your post with just one or two clicks of a mouse. Take note that even a person who wants to share your content may not be able to do so, unless you make the process of sharing easy and convenient for them. You can have your own sharing buttons by just using some HTML codes. If you want, you can also try sites like AddThis to provide you with cool share buttons.

About Me page

When you manage a blog, it is a good idea to have an About Me page. This is to make your readers feel more comfortable with you. This is also a way to reassure your visitors that they are connecting with a human being and not just a blog full of text. As you may already know, establishing a relationship with your readers is an important element to the success of any blog. Of course, to make such relationships possible, you readers must see you as the person you are, and an effective way to do that is to have an About Me page on your blog. Of course, do not forget to add a nice picture of yourself.

Contact page

Just like an About Me page, be sure that your blog has a Contact page, or any way that a reader can reach out to you. This is another good way to establish a relationship with your readers. You can expect to get messages from your blog readers from time to time. Although you do not have to answer right away, you should respond to the messages in about 48 hours. If you happen to get lots of messages, you can have a note on your Contact page that you want to answer all messages but may not be able to do so due to the high volume of messages that you receive. Then, include a short message saying that you appreciate everyone who sends you a message. As much as you can, try to respond to every email that you receive. This will be appreciated by your readers, even if your response takes more than a week. The important thing is to assure them that they are not being ignored.

Quantity vs. quality

You need to understand the importance of both the quality and quantity of your blog posts. Some people say that quality is more important than quantity. Although this is true, you should also take note that quantity is also important. A blog with just a few contents on the site will hardly draw enough attention from people, or keep followers. Therefore, focus on the quality as well as the quantity of your blog posts. Also, updating your blog regularly with new posts is another technique to increase your SEO rating and be more visible online. Keep in mind that blogging is a life-long journey, so feel free to add as many high-quality contents as you can.

Chapter 5: Putting It All Together

Now that you have the right knowledge and a perfect foundation on creating and managing a successful blog, it is time for you to put everything together into one solid strategy. Are you ready?

Maybe by now, you have a blog with some traffic trickling in daily. What do you do next? The key is simply to continue what you are doing. However, it is good if you come up with a particular goal. Even just a simple, easy to reach goal is better than nothing. For example, set a goal to increase your blog traffic by 30% within seven days.

You already know that there are many methods that you can use to drive traffic to your blog. You can guest post, write higher quality content, participate in social media, use Fiverr, and so on. Pick one or two methods that you want to use and work on them to increase your blog's traffic.

Remember that you are not limited to just increase your traffic to 30%. Even if you see that you have already met your goal, continue your efforts until you finish the end of seven days. If you fail to meet your target, then examine the causes on why it failed. You can make adjustments and try again. In case you do meet your goal in the allotted time, then congratulate yourself and appreciate your small success. Remember that a grand success is nothing but a series of small successes.

Establish a strong relationship

By now, you already know the importance of building a good rapport with other people. When you put things together, it is time to build a strong and lasting relationship with those who will become your partners in the blogging industry. In this world, you need to help one another. You should also be helping your competitors. After all, even your competitors can help promote your blog. In fact, your competitors can significantly help you in this area. This is true, especially if you establish a good relationship with them. Just imagine how much traffic you can get if your competitor announces your blog on their own site? Of course, you can also reciprocate the action. Instead of looking at your competitors as an enemy, you should strive to build a mutual relationship with them.

Establishing a good relationship is not just limited to your competitors. You should also have a good relationship with your blog visitors. If you follow all the pieces of advice in this book, then you can easily build a relationship with them, especially to those who actively interact with your blog posts.

Establish your expertise

As you continue to work on your blog, you should also focus on being an expert in your niche. Make sure that your blog covers all possible topics, and strive to be an authority in your respective field. Of course, there is no magical formula on how to establish your authority except by posting really good content, and demonstrating your knowledge and expertise. There is, however, another strategy to establish authority. You should be connected with those that already have authority on your subject. By connecting, discussing, and being on par with them, people will also consider you as an expert.

Establish a positive routine

It is shown that people do not like getting stuck in a routine. However, when you blog, it is not uncommon to do almost the same thing over and over again. To avoid getting bored, you can come up with different sets of routines. For example, for five days, you can focus on creating new content for the blog. Then for the next five days, you can focus on promoting your blog. You can follow it up with increasing your connections on social media. The key is to have a routine that will bring in positive developments or changes to your blog. As repeated throughout this book, blogging is a life-long journey. Just like any other lifestyle or career, create ways to avoid becoming stagnant.

Dedication and commitment

Your dedication and commitment to your blog will be tested now and again. Many times, you will be tempted to throw up your hands and abandon your blog. However, a good blogger knows that such temptations are usual challenges faced by everyone. During such times, remain true to your commitment to your blog. If you do have a feeling of walking away, take a day off to re-group yourself. Think about what happened to lead to this point in your journey. Then, begin taking steps to overcome the challenge and continue blogging. Always remember that you are never alone in feeling like this, and you will find a way around it.

Create another blog

You are not limited to just a single blog. Many successful bloggers manage several blogs at the same time. After all, it is really hard to tell which blog will be able to bring in a big amount of profit. You simply have to experiment and see what happens. Feel free to consider the idea of creating another blog. Do not be concerned about abandoning your old blog. Branching out to other topics in another niche could even help with burn out from the other.

If you want, you can come up with two blogs. The first blog can be a blog that you will manage solely to share your passion with the world, while you can use the other blog with a clear objective of generating money.

Having another blog can also be helpful in promoting your other blog/blogs. This strategy is highly effective, especially your readers do not know that the different blogs have the same author. You can always create a pen name.

Experiment

Experimenting will always lead to improving your blog. There is really no clear-cut way to come up with a blog that will give you thousands of dollars per month. Blogging is a journey; and like any other journey, it involves taking risks and meeting failures. Do not limit yourself with what you read online or what books say about blogging. In its fullest meaning, remember that blogging is about you. Do not be afraid to try new things on your own. It is your blog. Make it as beautiful as you want.

Take a break

Do not forget to give yourself time to rest and re-group. Blogging can be tiring, even as a hobby. There are simply so many things that you need to work on, such as acquiring a blog, designing it, answering comments, working on promotions, creating new content on a regular basis, editing, researching, and many others. These things can get tiring in the long run. So, learn to enjoy small successes, and give yourself a break.

5 Traits of Highly Successful Bloggers

By now, you may have already realized that there is really no secret as to what makes a blog successful. There is no secret ingredient to any blogging success story. You simply have to try and see it for yourself. There are, however, certain traits that successful bloggers have in common. You will usually notice these things when you examine their blogs closely. Although these traits do not in any way guarantee success, they are the traits or attitudes that top bloggers have:

Perseverance

Visit all the best bloggers, and you will see how they have persevered to reach the point of success that they have now. It is also nice to check on their oldest posts, so you can see the difference and the development they went through. Pay attention to their articles. See how much effort they have put into their blog. Even though they are already very successful, they still continue to update their blog regularly.

Patience

You can check all the popular blogs out there, and you can be assured that these blogs did not reach the point of success within a short period of time. In the same way, you should be patient with your blog. Take note that growth and development take time. You need to exercise patience. You cannot expect for your blog to start earning thousands of dollars in just a week or two, with these kinds of successes being very rare.

Helpful

Successful bloggers always post contents that can be truly helpful to their readers. They do not upload a new post just for the sake of uploading something. They always have something helpful or interesting to share. Do not underestimate the power of blogging. Your blog has the potential to help countless of people around the globe.

Friendly

Go to any excellent blog, and you will see the blog author also active in the comment box. Successful bloggers establish a good relationship with their visitors or readers. They make sure that they reply to every message politely and respectfully. They also ask their readers for suggestions and listen to them. They connect with their readers not just on the blog itself, but even on social media and via email. They tend to create friendships and lasting relationships.

Continuous improvement

Successful bloggers always strive for continuous improvement. They always seek for ways to improve their content. They do not stay within their comfort zone for long, knowing that getting stuck in one's comfort zone would restrict development. Even though they are already successful, they still remain up to date with the latest trends in blogging. In fact, they continue to do the things that they used to do even when they were not yet as successful. After all, the blogging world is a competitive place. You need to strive for continuous improvement and growth to have a steady stream of traffic and profits.

Conclusion

Congratulations on reaching the end of this book. We hope it was informative and able to provide you with all of the tools and know-how you need to achieve your goals, whatever they may be.

The next step is to apply everything that you have learned. So, go create a blog today and start this amazing journey! We wish you all the success you seek.

Finally, if you found this book useful, a review on Amazon is always appreciated!

Happy Blogging!

Description

How YOU Can Make Money Blogging from Home - The Ultimate Beginner's guide to turning your passion for blogging into paychecks using Proven strategies, tips and tricks: Taking you from beginner to pro with our step by step formula, you will learn how to setup your blog, design it, monetize it, and grow it! is your one-stop guide to everything that you need to know about blogging.

This handy manual will teach you the ins and outs of blogging, as well as how you can effectively turn your blog into a goldmine.

Learn:

- What a blog is

- How to make money with your blog

- How to create a blog

- The best blogging practices that you should observe

- How to generate more blog traffic

- How to increase your blog's visibility

- Effective strategies

And so much more!

What's inside the book?

Chapter 1 discusses the basics of blogging. It is vital to build a good base before you begin, so that you have a better understanding of what blogging really is, as well as to be informed about terminology and what goes into a blog.

Chapter 2 talks about the effective ways to make money with your blog. This is the key to generate profits, which can eventually lead to financial freedom.

Chapter 3 explains the ways you can draw traffic to your blogs, such as by taking advantage of social media and other outlets that promote blogs like yours.

Chapter 4 shares a number of tips and tricks that can significantly increase your chances of success. In the world of blogging, these are must-know tips that every successful blogger uses.

Chapter 5 shows you how to take what you have learned and apply it to your own blog.